Tyrone and Tyra

World of Discovery of Black Inventors

by

Jennifer Lenny

MAPLE
PUBLISHERS

Tyrone and Tyra – World of Discovery of Black Inventors

Author: Jennifer Lenny

Copyright © Jennifer Lenny (2024)

The right of Jennifer Lenny to be identified as author of this work has been asserted by the author in accordance with section 77 and 78 of the Copyright, Designs and Patents Act 1988.

First Published in 2024

ISBN 978-1-83538-130-4 (Paperback)
   978-1-83538-131-1 (E-Book)

Book Cover, Illustrations and Layout by:
   White Magic Studios
   www.whitemagicstudios.co.uk

Published by:
   Maple Publishers
   Fairbourne Drive, Atterbury,
   Milton Keynes,
   MK10 9RG, UK
   www.maplepublishers.com

A CIP catalogue record for this title is available from the British Library.

The book is a work of fiction. Unless otherwise indicated, all the names, characters, places and incidents are either the product of the author's imagination or used in a fictitious manner. Any resemblance to actual people living or dead, events or locales is entirely coincidental, and the Publisher hereby disclaims any responsibility for them.

All rights reserved. No part of this book may be reproduced or translated by any form or by any means, electronic or mechanical, including photocopying, recording or by any information storage and retrieval system without written permission from the author.

Aspiration and determination can help you achieve your goals. Never stop learning.

Betty Campbell
1934-2017

Acknowledgements

I would like to make a tribute to Betty Campbell (MBE). Betty Campbell was born in Butetown, also known as Cardiff Bay in South Wales, UK in 1937.

She was Wales' first black Head teacher. She made Mount Stuart Primary School in Cardiff, UK, a model for multi-cultural education in Britain. She was appointed MBE - Member of the British Empire - in 2003.

I was also born in Butetown, Cardiff UK, same area as Betty Campbell. Her statue can be seen outside the BBC in Cardiff, South Wales, UK.

Betty was a champion of education. I am happy to have known her. She was a pioneer who inspired people. One of aspiration and inspiration. This statue speaks volumes of this remarkable black lady.

Chapter 1

Welcome to The World of Black Inventors

Summer was finally here. Tyrone and Tyra were packing their suitcases, ready for their summer holiday to Florida, Disneyland.

The twins were very excited. "This will be great fun", they exclaimed as they put all their clothes into the suitcase.

"Are you both ready?" they heard a voice up the stairs. It was mum wanting to know if they were ready.

"Almost" the twins replied.

Tyrone and Tyra were eleven years old and they were very intelligent for their age.

"Let's play a game of Black inventors" Tyra suggested.

"That's a great idea," Tyrone said.

The house needed a last check before they made their way out through the door.

"Let's start with the ironing board. This needs to be put away." "Who invented the ironing board?" Tyrone said to Tyra.

"In 1892, it was a lady named Sarah Brooke," Tyra said. "Now let's move on to packing the drinks for our journey."

"Who invented the bottle top?" Tyra counter-questioned Tyrone.

"In 1899, Robert Reynolds invented the bottle top," Tyrone replied. "Jolly good," Tyra declared.

"Have you packed our water guns?" Tyra asked!

"Yes," Tyrone confirmed.

"Who was the inventor of the water guns?" Tyrone asked Tyra.

"I know it was an inventor by the name of Loni Johnson, in 1982."

"Yes! That's correct Tyra."

"This game of knowledge is so much fun!" the twins commented at the same time. Tyrone and Tyra were twins. They were always playing a game of knowledge which gave them much understanding of the world in which we live.

"We need to set the Burglar Alarm. Let's not forget to set it," they both chorussed.

"Tyra, who invented the Burglar Alarm?"

"Mary Van Brittan Brown was the inventor, in 1966. She was also granted a patent for her work."

"WOW WEE!! You got that right!" Tyrone commented.

Now last of all, we need to switch the lights off before we exit the house.

"Who was the inventor of the light bulb Tyrone?" Tyra said.

"It was Lewis Latimer, in 1881."

"GEE WHIZ!" Tyra commented, "You got that right! We are all set to go now."

Mum and Dad were outside in the car waiting for the twins.

Chapter 2

We Are Off to Disneyland Florida

"Holy Macaroni" the twins exclaimed at once.

"We are on our way to the airport to Disneyland in Florida. This will be so much fun!"

"Hurry up!" Mum ordered, "We don't want to be late!"

The twins got into the back seat of the car, buckled up, while Dad placed their luggage in the boot of the car.

Dad started the engine, all his mirror check done and so the car was in gear, ready to drive off.

"Tyra, do you know who invented the automatic gear shift?" Tyrone asked.

"Yes, I do know. It was Richard Spikes, in 1932."

"Jolly GOOD! You got that correct, Tyra," Tyrone commented. "I know that you didn't forget. Just testing your knowledge."

They drove past the park where they used to play with their friends – Callum and Ellexus. The twins were both looking through the window hoping that they would spot their friends, Callum and Ellexus, in the Pickersgill Park.

"I can see them on the slide. Let's wave to them. Oh! They are waving back! They can see us. Awesome!!!" the twins burst out.

The twins waved with a big smile as they drove up a 20 mile per hour zone. Then the car started to slow down as they approached the traffic lights.

"I've got one question for you Tyrone," Tyra said. "Who invented the safety brakes on the car?"

"It was invented in 1902 by Richard Bowie Spikes."

"WOW WEE! Perfect!" Tyra declared.

"Now your turn, Tyra. Who invented the traffic lights?"

"I know," Tyra declared. "It was Garrett Morgan, in 1923. He was also granted a patent for his invention."

"Jolly GOOD!" Tyrone stated. "You got that right. Let's watch a Marvel Adventure on our tablet," he said to Tyra.

"Great idea!"

They brought out their tablets and tuned in to their favourite Spider Man movies. "That was good," they both proclaimed, "Greatest of all times!"

Chapter 3

The Service Station Toilet Break

The summer breeze blew through the car window. The air was fresh and clean. The twins had fallen asleep after watching their favourite Marvel Adventure.

They were woken up by Mum's gentle voice. "Time to wake up, twins," she called. "We are now going to have a toilet break at the service station. We will then continue our journey."

"I can't wait to use the toilet," Tyrone said as they drove in at the service station.

"Super Duper!" Tyra said.

The queue was quite short, so the twins were in and out before they knew it.

"That was Boujee! (Actually funny)," Tyra said.

"I bet you don't know who invented the Modern Toilets."

"Yes, I do," Tyrone replied. "The inventor was a man called Thomas Elkins (1872). He may not have invented the toilet outright, but his improvement to the working order of the toilet was inspired. He was granted a patent. His designs came with several additional features such as – Mirrors, Hand wash stand, the Toilet Water Tank. The Valve System was added later was added to get the toilet up and running in the way we have it today. So there, you have it."

"That's awesome!" Tyra gushed.

"I've got one for you, Tyra," Tyrone stated. "Who invented the toilet holder?"

"I know it was two sisters, Mary Beatrice Davidson Kenner (1970's) together with her sister. They shared the patent."

"GEE WHIZZ!!! You got that right Tyra!"

"Super Duper!" Tyrone responded.

Chapter 4
Sing Songs on the way to the Airport

The twins' Mum and Dad were now back inside their vehicle, ready to continue their journey to the airport.

"Let's have a sing song," Tyrone said to Tyra.

"What are we going to sing?" Tyra queried.

"I know one of our best and favourite, Michael Jackson's, songs."

"Great idea," Tyra agreed.

"Let's sing together," Tyrone declared to his sister. "OK!" Tyra said.

"Let's start with the 'Brain' song, Tyrone."

What about sunsets?

What about pain?

What about all the things that you said we were to brain?

Chorus: Aaach!! Oooh!! Aaach!!

"How about another one, Tyra?" Tyrone said.

"Yes, let's sing 'Need the World', Tyra said, "Another Micheal Jackson's song."

"Yes, why not!" Tyrone replied. "How about 'Need the world'?"

"Yes that's great!!" they both agreed. "Let's go."

Need the World

There's a slot in your home and I know that it's loved.

And this home. It was brighter than a sparrow

Chorus: ... Need the World.

"We will be at the airport soon! I just saw a sign saying 'Heathrow Airport – Welcome'," Tyra stated.

The twins were very excited. They had never visited Disneyland in Florida. Before they had done doing some research on the rides. Also, everything that Disneyland has to offer, beforehand.

Chapter 5

We are at the airport

"We are finally here!" they commented.

"Time to check in our luggage, twinnies," Mum said.

The airport was full of excited passengers travelling to different parts of the world. People rushing to stand in line, to check-in their luggage and get to their gate number. Some were just relaxing in the Bar Lounge. Others shopping in the duty-free shops.

"It's all done now," Dad said, "we can go straight to Gate number 3 for our flight. The flight is due to take off soon."

The steward and stewardesses were at the gate ready to take their tickets and boarding passes. The twins found their seat numbers on the flight and made themselves comfortable. After 30 minutes, the plane was ready to take-off.

"GEE WIZZ!!!" Tyrone commented, "We are finally flying!"

"Wow Wee!" Tyra said, "This is exciting!"

They were finally flying. The sky was clear blue. The clouds looked like white candy floss, just floating past their tiny windows.

"Yay! This is exciting!" Tyra said.

Chapter 6

On The Plane and Planning For Destination

"Tyrone," Tyra asked, "do you know who invented the aeroplane propeller?"

"Umm…. Let me think… Yes, I know!" Tyrone declared.

"In 1920, the inventor was a man called James E. Hanger. He was also granted a patent for his invention."

"Jolly Good! You got that one right," Tyra replied.

The flight would take at least 7 hours. The twins kept themselves entertained by watching their favourite movie. This time they decided to watch 'Black Panther'. They had also done some reading and talking about what they would have to do once they arrived at their destination.

The journey went quite quick as the twins kept themselves entertained.

"We must download the *My Experience App* which is going to be our best friend," Tyrone stated, "All the best shows and adventures would be found on the App."

"Great thinking!" Tyra said.

"Let's not forget, we have to purchase a Disney Photo Pass for the duration of our trip. The Disney Memory Maker – it will be a great way to take beautiful photos of us while we are here. We can give them as gifts to Callum and Ellexus, when we return from our trip."

"Great thinking, Tyrone!" Tyra said.

Chapter 7

Hotel Arrival

The captain of the plane announced that the plane would be landing soon. The bulbs above their heads had shown a flashing light. The plane was going to touch down in 30 minutes.

"Buckle up twinnies!" Mum said to the twins, "we are about to land shortly."

"This is going to be a lot of fun!" the twins said to each other.

"Yes, cool!" Tyra said, "We have landed safely."

"Time to collect our luggage and head for the hotel," Dad added.

"Wow Wee Tyrone!" Tyra commented, "We are finally in Disneyland!"

The coach was waiting to take them to the hotel, outside the airport.

"Come on, Tyra," Tyrone said, "the coach is here and waiting for us."

Chapter 8

This is Just Magical

The coach ride to the hotel was a short ride.

There wasn't much to see, just the motorway and passing cars.

The coach had now reached its destination. It was the moment of excitement. The twins gathered all their belongings and stepped out of the coach. The hotel was right there in front of them. Their eyes opened wide like saucers.

"GEE WIZZ Tyrone," Tyra exclaimed, "This is just magical."

As they entered the doors to the hotel reception they were greeted by Minnie and Mickey Mouse characters. And a photo was taken on the spot.

They checked-in at the reception desk and were given the keys to their rooms. They had to go up a lift to get to the 12th floor to where they were staying.

Tyrone asked Tyra, "Do you know who invented the elevator?" as they entered.

"Yes! Of course! I know," Tyra replied, "it was a man by the name of Alexander Miles, in 1887. Not only did he invent the elevator, he was also in the 'National Inventors' Hall of Fame'."

"GEE WIZZ Tyra!" Tyrone proclaimed, "You remembered all of this!"

"Yep!" Tyra responded.

Chapter 9

More Inventions

The rooms of the twins were facing the swimming pools of the Disneyland complex.

"We must use this pool while we are here," Tyra suggested as she looked through the window, "our water guns will come in handy."

"Yes!" Tyrone responded, "This will be so much fun!"

"Let's go to get something to eat once we have unpacked," Dad told.

"Great idea!" the twins agreed.

"Oh! Look Tyrone!" Tyra stated, "We have folding beds. Do you know who invented the folding bed?" Tyra asked.

"Yes!" Tyrone replied, "It was Sarah E. Goode, in 1885. She was also granted a patent for her invention."

"Jolly good!" Tyra appreciated.

Chapter 10

Exploring Disneyland

Tyra and Tyrone got a Disney Map to help them get around the complex. Disneyland is made up of four parks –

(1) Magic Kingdom

(2) EPCOT centre

(3) Disney Hollywood Studios

    and

(4) Disney Animal Kingdom

The twins were staying at the Deluxe Resort Hilton Hotel. They were provided with free transportation (bus) to get them to and from their hotel to the parks.

"Time for something to eat," Mum and Dad declared.

"Yummy, yummy!" the twins chorused, "Let's go."

The twins looked at their Disney map and discovered that they weren't too far away from Liberty Square. They had some refreshments and a healthy snack and were ready to discover what Disneyland had to offer.

Liberty Square, they found was very educational. It takes you straight back to the 'Colonial Era of the United States' right in the midst of the Revolutionary War.

"Ellexus and Callum would enjoy this," Tyrone said to Tyra, "they love all things history."

"They sure do," Tyra said, "let's take loads of photos, so that we can show them when we return home."

Next was the Peter Pan's Flight. This flight took the twins on a high flying adventure over iconic scenes. This Ride was made famous by the Disney animated film – Peter Pan.

What fun they had! They even got to fly over London, where Big Ben and Tower bridge light up the night.

"This is so magical!" Tyra said to Tyrone, who was dazzled by the excitement of the whole ride and experience.

"Let's go on to the carousel of progress," Tyra said to Tyrone.

"Yes! Yes! Yes! We are having so much fun!" Tyrone was just in his elements.

They watched a family of 4 generations progress. How technology transforms their lives over a period of time!

"This is Boujee!" Tyra said after the ride.

Then they visited 'Tomorrowland'. They were shown – how the world is moving towards the future.

"Wow! Wee!" Tyrone exclaimed, "I'm just having so much fun!"

"Me too!" agreed Tyra, "this is very educational."

"Let's head to the gift shop, Tyrone," Tyra suggested. "Great idea," Tyrone said.

The gift shop was at Bonjour village. There were lots of gifts of many kinds – Mickey Mouse, hats, gloves, games, puzzles and many more.

"We must not forget to buy postcards."

"Yes Tyrone," Tyra said, "and also a pen to write them out. I just came up with another invention. Who invented the post box?" Tyra asked.

"It was Philip B. Downing, in 1891."

"Yes, that's perfect Tyrone! You got that right. Also who invented the fountain pen?"

"The inventor was a man named William Pervis, in 1890."

"Well done! Jolly good, Tyrone! That's just marvellous."

Mum and Dad wanted to take a break as the twins had had them walking around the park for hours.

"Let's take a break, Twinnies," Mum said to the twins.

"Who fancies a Macaron from Jely at the Holiday bakery Cafe? Then it will be time for night time fireworks."

"Yipeee!" The twins couldn't wait.

"What a fun-filled day we had!" Tyrone said to Tyra. "Tomorrow is another day."

Chapter 11

A World Of Knowledge

The Next Day...

The twins got up early as you have to be at the park at the crack of dawn to get the best of Disneyland. There were kids everywhere having a great time, with big smiles on their faces.

"Let's go to Fantasyland," Mum and Dad said to the twins. Everyone is a kid in Disneyland.

Fantasyland is like walking into tales from your childhood. It comes alive all around you – clowns, music and characters. There's just so much to see and do. In Disney the time flies when you are having fun.

The twins' holidays were almost over. They played in the swimming pool with their water guns, splashing around and spraying their guns at each other.

Now it was time to go back home.

"What great fun we had!" Tyra said to Tyrone as they packed to get ready.

"Yes, we sure did have lots of fun."

"What was your favourite?" Tyrone asked Tyra.

"The Royal Castle inspired by Beauty and the Beast. Also the Hall of Presidents. We were able to take a seat in the Stately Theatre with the 3 massive digital projection screens and it had a grand procession."

"I enjoyed walking around the lobby as we got to see the Memorabilia from Present to Past, great fun!"

"My favourite was," (said Tyra), "Adventure-land where we lived our dreams of an exotic adventure, fighting pirates and flying through an Arabian Market. Oh! What fun we had!"

"The Swiss family Robinson Tree House was amazing with breath-taking views." "I also enjoyed." (Tyra said). "We got to tour the Island that Swiss family Robinsons built. They were ship-wrecked on a deserted Island."

"Boujee! Fancy! That was enjoyable. What a world of adventure Disneyland is!"

TYRONE AND TYRA WERE HAVING FUN AND ENTERTAINMENT!

HOPE YOU ENJOYED THE JOURNEY.

AND KEEP LEARNING.

Also, patents enables the inventors to profit from sale and licences.

End Credit

Let us celebrate these black inventors who changed the world and made our daily life easier.

These Black inventors changed the world.

Not all inventions were granted patent due to oppression and discrimination. However, some inventors were recorded in the national inventors' HALL OF FAME for their inventions.

www.ingramcontent.com/pod-product-compliance
Lightning Source LLC
Chambersburg PA
CBHW051351110526
44591CB00025B/2971